ON THE NOSE

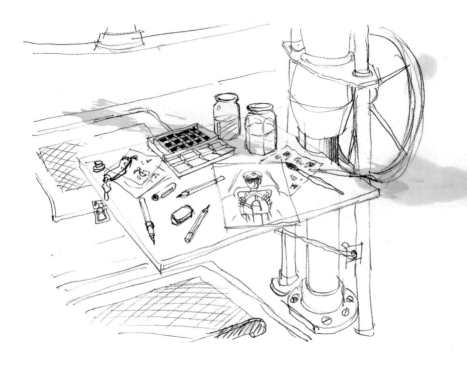

Written and illustrated by Bob Cooper

"I must go down to the sea again,
The lonely sea and the sky.
I left my shoes and socks there,
I wonder if they're dry?"

Spike Milligan

On the nose

A sideways look at cruising and living aboard in the Western Mediterranean

Written and illustrated by
Bob Cooper

© Bob Cooper 2008

Published in 2008 by:

Nosetheon Books, Ship to Shore, P O Box 400, Winchester, SO22 4RY

ISBN 978-0-9559256-0-3

Illustrations: Bob Cooper
Copy-editing: Andrew Morley
Design and typesetting: Bob Cooper
Image scanning and digitising: Liz Cooper
Text set digitally in Times New Roman
Printed by 1010, China on behalf of MBC Print

A CIP record for this book is available from the British Library.

Contents

For Liz

Yours is the wind beneath my sheets.

Introduction

Why you should buy this book

I don't quite know *who* will read this book. It'll probably be somebody who has a boat already, but not necessarily. I hope everybody would find it funny. Funny enough to buy as a gift maybe. That would broaden the market alright. But it's probably somebody who sails already, is dreaming about jacking the job in, giving the business suit and ties to Oxfam, and going off to sail a boat somewhere warm and sunny and where it's cheaper than staying at home.

And it is! Our last winter's entire marina fees were less than one month's standing orders for our house in England. You can live very cheaply and have a good time in a warm sunny climate. You will be the envy of your friends. Some of them may come to visit you. Some may be so jealous they'll never talk to you again. But that doesn't matter, you'll meet all sorts of interesting characters from all around the world, not just the ones down the pub.

The book is most relevant to the yachties on a budget, and there are a lot of us about. It's not a guide or a pilot or a how-to-do-it book, it's just about how *we* did it, the experiences we had along the way and the unexpected problems we had to conjure up solutions for.

If your boat is over 50 feet long or you've got a catamaran the size of the centre court at Wimbledon, then you've probably got the wherewithal to *buy* solutions to all those problems. You'll *have* Inmarsat. You'll *have* a full set of Minton china including six eggcups. You'll *have* electric winches, windlasses, electric flushing loos with motion-detecting air freshener puffers, climate control, broadband, wi-fi, dishwasher, laundromat, and a small Filipino boy to wipe the condensation off your deck each morning before he brings you an Earl Grey tea in bed in your master stateroom.

You may think this book is not for you, unless you like slumming it, or want to see how the other half lives, or your technology shares have nose-dived and you need to downsize your boat. But why not buy it anyway. I need the money after all.

Bob Cooper

1

Actually doing it

Actually, unequivocally, irrevocably, without a doubt, in no uncertain terms, unswervingly, with firm resolve, doing it. Going cruising. You've been telling everybody you were going to, so you really have to, don't you? Otherwise your credibility will hit rock bottom and nobody will believe a word you say ever again.

That's what we found anyway. I know you could argue that you could just say to people: 'Well, we'll just pop downriver to the estuary, then we'll see how it goes…'

But this response wears a bit thin after they've heard you banging on for years about the planning and preparation, and you know they've rumbled you and you just have to do it.

It's a bit like what we were told about crossing the Atlantic by Bill, a 75-year-old South African we met in Turkey, and *he* crossed from South Africa to Brazil in a boat he taught himself to build from books, using mail order materials, in the middle of the South African veldt: 'The hardest part was untying the mooring lines. Compared to that everything else was a doddle.'

And it's true. When we set off we thought we were embarking on a Great Adventure, and don't get me wrong, for us it certainly was. It was only when we got to the Med that we realised that there are *loads* of people doing it, in all sorts of boats and in all sorts of ways. There's a whole floating community of people in the Med from Gibraltar to Damascus who are all enjoying the same way of life, facing the same problems and helping each other overcome them, regardless of who they were, what they did, or how much they earned in the many years BC (Before Cruising) that they were stuck in the rat race.

So here's what you have to do…

First you have to learn to sail

You can learn a lot by sailing with more experienced yachtsmen. Try the Irish Sea in early May like we did.

Then there's the theory. There are evening classes in RYA Day Skipper and Yachtmaster all over the country where you can learn the finer points of seamanship. Liz and I were taught Day Skipper by Yvonne, a rare female Yachtmaster who was a great teacher. Organised, reliable, knew her stuff, in control. The only time she lost it was when, in response to asking how you would get a heavy, dripping wet, semi-conscious MOB (man overboard) back in the boat, the class clown immediately put his hand up saying 'Please Miss, please Miss.' This is a middle-aged man, not a 14-year-old schoolboy. 'Stick a gaff hook under his chin and hoick him up, Miss.'

Yvonne slid down her chair, snorting and giggling, all thoughts of safety procedure replaced by the absurd mental image presented to her. In fact she was probably thinking of her husband on the hook. He taught Yachtmaster down the corridor.

3

Then you'll need a boat

And very soon you'll meet your good friends The Yacht Broker and The Surveyor, stalwart sources of unbiased advice for anxious novice boat buyers undergoing a very stressful process (in other words, us).

The brokerage where we bought Yanina had a kind of schizophrenic approach to customer care. Partner Number 1, friendly, genial and garrulous, generously drove us from the airport to the brokerage. We began to enjoy ourselves. And then... we met Partner Number 2. After ignoring us for a good fifteen minutes, he leapt up, threw lifejackets at us and barked at us to follow him. Liz asked to use the toilet. Instantly motionless, the only movement a tic in his cheek, he considered this request.

'I. Suppose. Possible. Yes.'

The words flowed like bullets from a jammed Kalashnikov. The key was found. We walked to the shed next door, avoiding any sudden movements.

'What do you think?' I murmured.

'Barking,' said Liz. 'You keep him talking, I'll go for help.'

After a body-search for bits of copper pipe and toilet seats, we zoomed off in a RIB in an arcing curve of spray. The big shiny outboard motor sputtered, stopped, and stayed stopped. TYB started up the rather more modest spare motor, and we puttered sedately off. A tired old ketch and an exhausted old motorsailer convinced us that we'd wasted a day and a flight and here we were stuck in a rubber dinghy in the middle of a lough and what if the spare motor packed up as well, when he said, 'Ha. Got. Another. Came in. Yesterday. Might be for you.'

This was his longest sentence so far. Things were. Looking. Up.

We approached Yanina. She looked like a proper yacht, nice hull shape, in good nick, aft cabin accessed from the big centre cockpit. Having seen lots of Moody's with enormous aft cabins reached by sauntering along endless corridors in the warm and dry ('Turn right at the chart table, carry on past the engine room, and it's just at the end there. Can't miss it.') I didn't fancy a separate aft cabin in the pouring rain. But this boat made sense. A winter canopy completely covered the deep centre cockpit, zipped onto the big wide sprayhood. A conservatory! We unzipped our way in and climbed down into the saloon.

TYB remained crouching on deck so we didn't feel too crowded (Tip Number 47 in the Yacht Brokers' Customer Care Handbook). A Warrior 35's saloon is better described as an alcove with a table in it where you can eat your dinner. In fact you don't even have to get out of your seat on top of the fridge to open the oven door. Lean to the left a bit and you can almost do the washing-up. Lean to the right and you can work out your next route on the chart table.

But TYB had prepared his ground. The table was slid right up to the top of its pole, apparently doubling the space below.

'Just look at the space will ye. Sure, ye could hold a dance down there.'

We looked at him. He looked away, intently examining one of the two elderly winches, letting this helpful and informative observation sink in. Fortunately for him and us, he didn't have to say any more. Liz grabbed my arm and whispered:

'This is it!'

'Is it? But it's not even on my spreadsheet of Yachts We Might Possibly Consider Buying Even Though We Can't Ever Afford Them.'

Liz tightened her grip on my arm. Her eyes widened. I recognised the signs. This was it. Love.

'Sod the spreadsheet. Let's make an offer.'

And so we did.

And then you'll need an independent surveyor

In order to get a totally independent and unbiased opinion on the boat, we of course asked TYB to recommend a local surveyor. A bit like a Christmas turkey asking the way to Sainsbury's, but we didn't have a lot of choice. Time was running out, money was running out, we were stressed out. We needed a boat.

Our Surveyor had clearly weathered a few hundred gales. Broken veins competed with tufts of grey hair for space on his wind-blasted cheeks. A battered peaked cap shaded a pair of bewrinkled twinkly eyes.

He prowled and sniffed his way around the boat, and we followed, anxiously looking for any signs of a problem: the sucking-in of air over the teeth, the odd tut-tut. Inside, the large windows in the forecabin had curtains all round them. He swished and rattled them.

'See Bawb, big winders here. Be sure you keep these curtains eh? Ye don't want people looking in at you, do ye?' he winked.

'What about the engine?' I ventured. It was after all 27 years old and could be expensive to replace.

'Ach! I don't do engines.' he snapped.

It was at this point that the words 'up' and 'stitched' were elbowing their way into my thoughts. It's not that I'm paranoid, it's just that both my psychotherapist (or 'brain mechanic' as she likes to be called) and I agree that they're all out to get me. At the last panto I went to, when the audience shouted 'He's behind you!' I had to leave the theatre.

A few more sniffs and deft scrapes to the antifouling with a Boy Scout's penknife, and the survey was complete. Yanina was pronounced healthy.

'What ye need to do now, Bawb, is to spend nothin' on her for at least a year, till ye know what ye really need.'

Good advice, I thought.

'Not even new curtains?'

In response he winked and walked off, no doubt to find the Boy Scout so he could give him his penknife back. We didn't need to worry. He knew his stuff and he knew Yanina. He'd surveyed her the year before.

So what sort of boat had we bought?

In the 1960s and '70s, boats were on the whole slimmer than they are now, a bit like us. But unlike us, while we were in purple velvet flares and lime green paisley kaftans, they had sensible long generous keels into which a good few tons of molten lead had been poured, so they could move more or less in a straight line in spite of what the wind and waves were doing to them. And if they heeled over, they still sailed in a straight line - it was all in the hull shape. This was gently curved and tapered at both ends. So unlike a boat with a modern hull shape it didn't slam down off a wave into the next trough, waves from behind didn't slap it's bottom noisily, and it didn't wobble or creak because it was made of *thick* fibreglass, thoroughly soaked in polyester resin lovingly laid in by hand by a bloke in overalls. This was all before we had oil crises, you see, so they just slapped the layers on till it felt thick enough and didn't worry too much about the money. That of course is why they don't make them any more. They went bust.

And most people didn't go into marinas then, mainly because there weren't any. They just anchored. So steering a straight line in reverse just wasn't an issue.

Yanina, who was born in 1977, has all these qualities. Straight line ahead? No problem, she sails herself if you get the sails set right. But she won't tell you where she's going in reverse, she needs a good steady 15 knots of wind to get sailing, and you can forget ballroom dancing in the saloon, she only has about two-thirds the space inside compared with a wide-bodied modern mass-produced cruiser. 'Ooh, how cosy!' say most of our first-time visitors. But at least you won't get thrown across an expanse of floor into the sink when a big 'greenie' (unexpectedly large wave) has its evil way with her.

Just what is it that makes Yanina the ideal cruising boat?

A   **50 watt solar panel** Never quite supplies enough juice to run the fridge

B   **Wind generator** Frustratingly for the sailor, this does not generate wind, unlike the crew. It doesn't generate much electricity either

C   **Over the side/the upstairs toilet** Only use when firmly attached to the boat. Many of the corpses found washed ashore have their flies undone

D   **Boom** To hang sun awning from

E   **Wheel** Grip here in times of stress

F   **Guard rail** To tie sun awning to, and to lean over when chundering

G   **Pole** For lap dancers, what else?

H   **Mast** To hold boom at correct height for sun awning

I   **Heads** Go here in times of extreme stress

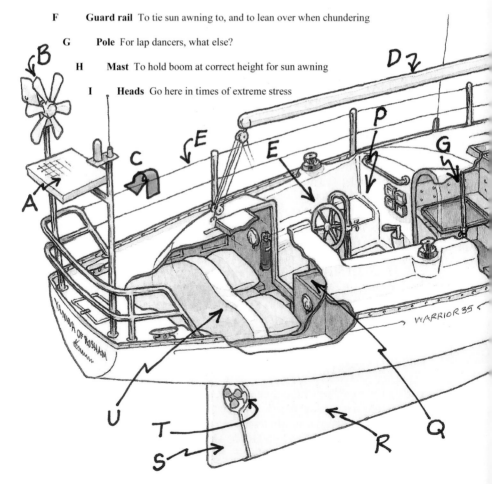

J   **Toe rail** For stubbing toes on

K   **Pulpit** For preaching to other yachties

L   **Forward cabin** Handy for lying awake listening to anchor chain rumbling on seabed

M   **Mould incubation chamber** Also known as the wardrobe

N   **Galley** Where I wander around looking for scraps of food until Liz takes pity on me

O   **Chart table** Where we try to find out where we'll be tomorrow. Contains charts, dice, tarot cards and crystal ball

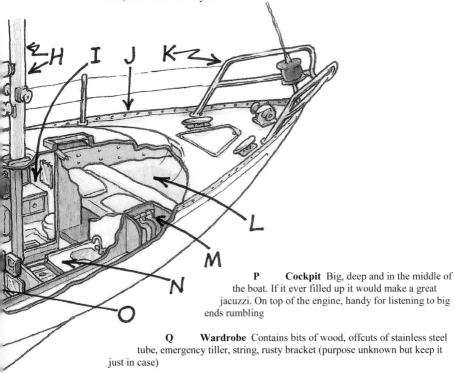

P   **Cockpit** Big, deep and in the middle of the boat. If it ever filled up it would make a great jacuzzi. On top of the engine, handy for listening to big ends rumbling

Q   **Wardrobe** Contains bits of wood, offcuts of stainless steel tube, emergency tiller, string, rusty bracket (purpose unknown but keep it just in case)

R   **Long keel** Essential feature to prevent reversing and steering at the same time

S   **Rudder** May have something to do with steering

T   **Stern gland** Emits an oily secretion by which other Warrior 35's can recognise Yanina

U   **Aft cabin** Handy for lying awake listening to wind generator rumbling. When unoccupied, known as the bike shed

But since we want to go further than the Med, we're glad we got her. We keep meeting people who say things like: 'Ah, Warrior 35... took mine round the world in '83, got knocked down off Papua New Guinea, rolled straight up again.' Or 'Went right over a floating whale in '79 off the Tuamotus, never felt a thing. Whale never woke up either.' I don't know whether they were trying to reassure us or give us the screaming ab-dabs.

But if you're planning to stay in the Med for good, and you don't want a motor boat, then you need something a bit lighter, with a wide beam so you've got lots of room inside, a big fridge, in-mast reefing on the main so that you don't wear yourself out taking reefs in and out every ten minutes in the flukey wind shifts, an aft cockpit with a big table and a huge bimini, a sugar scoop stern that you can swim off and shower on, and a short keel so you can turn on a sixpence and back up into your marina berth in 20 knots of side wind.

But get your sails down sharpish in the 'forts raffalés', or you'll be laid on your ear before you can say 'Bavaria'.

And then you have to pay for the boat

You may decide you want to do this by selling your house and possibly everything else you can't take on board. This gives some yachties a tremendous sense of freedom, and gives others the willies.

The latter are the ones that hang grimly onto the property ladder with one hand, while steering the boat with the other. They rent their house out, generously giving the bulk of their proceeds to support local business, in the form of their letting agents, their plumbers, roofers, painters, electricians and washing machine repair men. This is what we did, and our letting agents are eternally grateful to us for radically improving their profitability status.

But whether you're a Sell-up-and-Sailor or a Seafarer-Landlord, you eventually reach the point where you lock the door on your past life, squeeze into the car, crammed with last-minute gear and things-that-might-just-come-in-handy, and set off. This is the moment of truth, when you realise just what you've been and gone and done.

Preparing the boat

While we did do a few things over the first winter in Scotland to get Yanina ready for our trip (we never did change the curtains), most of the preparation was done on the way, as and when we found out what we really needed.

Like radar

There's more chance of finding a bacon sandwich in Turkey than meeting fog in the Med, but there's plenty of it along the way. So radar is very handy.

And anyway, you'll be doing some night sailing, so on the way to the Med it's quite reassuring to see all those unlit Portuguese fishing boats, invisible to the eye, revealed as dots on the screen.

If you've got the time and patience, and all the right tools, fit the radar yourself. If you've got less time and more sense, get a man in.

Fine-tuning the radar installation

Or bikes

We think bikes are a high priority for the Med. When you get into port, you can go much further much quicker, you can avoid such pavement obstacles as time-share touts and beckoning waiters, you can lug your shopping back on the handlebars, or if your guests are getting bored from being stuck on board while you're hiding from gales, you can give them a set of wheels for the day to relieve the tedium.

What sort of bike?

Most yachties buy folding bikes. We researched all the magazine articles and measured our locker lids, and even though each cockpit locker is big enough to swallow up a Harley Davidson, none of the bikes seemed to fold small enough to cram in through the small opening. So, another problem to be solved along the way. But then in Padstow, we found a couple of ex-hire mountain bikes for sale, very cheap. The wheels were quick-release, and *did* fit in the lockers. The frames could be tied on deck.

The pedals, at any rate one of them, were not-so-quick-release, until this bicycle technology consultant gave us some free advice.

A sewing machine

If you've got one, take your sewing machine with you (well, maybe not this one). It doesn't matter a great deal if it's mains-operated; you can always nip into a marina for power, or you might be able to run it from an inverter if you have one.

Liz made this bag for the bike frames from an old windsurfer sail. It's handy for lowering them into the dinghy too when you're at anchor.

Wheels and pedals in cockpit locker→

15

Once you've got your sewing machine on board, other jobs just emerge. For example, you don't have to spend a fortune on boat-shaped bedding at the Boat Show. You can do it yourself and pay for a couple of your winter months in the marina on the savings.

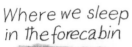

Where we sleep in the forecabin

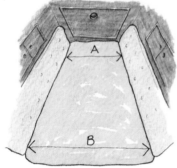

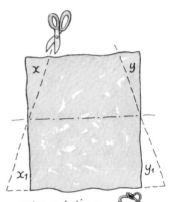

The problem:
1. 'B' is much bigger than 'A'
2. Bedding is rectangular

The solution:
1. cut off 'x' and 'y'
2. sew on at 'x₁' and 'y₁'
3. sleep on it (or under it)

Liz has also repaired sails, replaced zips on sail covers, made cockpit seat covers, and most importantly, made a soft padded bag for my guitar from some very ethnic fabric. We bought it in a shop in Turkey, in my next book, 'Right on the nose' (see last page of this one for details).

Musical instruments

Talking of guitars, or indeed of any musical instrument, if you've got one take it with you. It's amazing how many musicians are lurking in boats just waiting for a chance to show off, and with a captive audience of entertainment-starved yachties roaming the marina bars, there's all winter to indulge.

We've got two guitars, a clarinet, an alto sax, a mike and stand, a busker's amp and a tambourine. On other boats I've seen trombones, full-size electronic keyboards, multi track mixing desks, and I met one ex-professional drummer selling off anchors, rope and fenders, determined to find a space for a full drum kit. There's commitment for you...

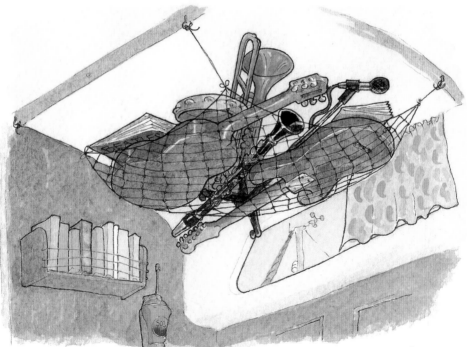

Safe storage of musical instruments is essential...

Storage

We put nets up wherever we can; however much the boat rolls nothing ever falls out. The secret is to have a minimum of three hooks, otherwise you've made a miniature hammock. Hopeless.

Nets are not just for the guitars and woodwind, but for fruit and veg in the galley, and for our drawing pads and modelling card in the aft cabin.

And bungee, or shock cord, is your elastic friend who will hold you tight in all sorts of places. The stylish and funky loudspeaker, by the way,

is one of a pair engineered to extremely high specification from a couple of car speakers and two transparent plastic storage jars with white lids from a Spanish supermarket. Very iPod. Very Yanina.

Improvisation

But if you forgot the sewing machine, don't worry, just improvise.

This handsome and rather fetching outboard motor cover was seen on a boat in Corsica. British of course.

Could any other nation spawn such ingenious ad hoc design, such original thinking or such elegantly simple problem-solving ability? Don't talk to me about Italian design, that lot don't know the first thing.

To protect the outboard motor from the sun, you don't have to buy a special cover....

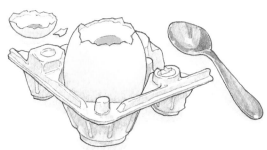

Instant disposable eggcup

And if you've forgotten the set of Minton china egg-cups just get the scissors out... smooth or what?

Seasickness

So the boat's all sorted, but what about the crew? Seasickness, mal-de-mer, the technicolour yawn, the old chunder. Call it what you will, for lots of people it's the biggest problem to overcome. You can learn all your knots, figure out all your nav, or spring off a berth in a brisk breeze, but if you can't hang on to your breakfast, you're going to be pretty miserable. But then…

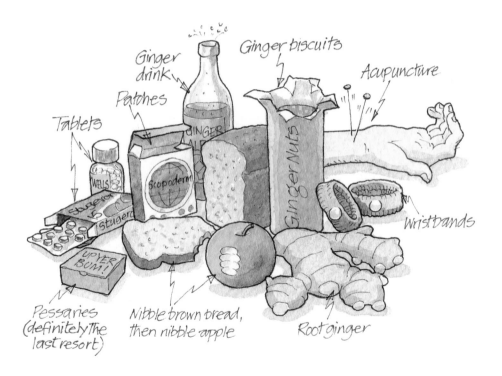

…there are all sorts of remedies you can try, some more radical than others, and perhaps best self-administered. By the way, it's only the pessaries that can be used as per the instructions on the pack. Don't try it with any of the other remedies, particularly the root ginger.

And there are techniques for reducing your susceptibility. Seasickness is about the conflict between what your various senses, mainly sight and balance, are telling your brain. Cut one out, and you reduce the conflict. Liz swears that when you go below, if you keep your eyes closed while you get undressed until you can lie down, you'll be fine.

She still has a few problems to solve when she has to get dressed again and go back on watch.

21

I used to get seasick very easily. I've tried quite a few cures. I've made myself so dozy with tablets I was too tired to throw up, so I guess that's a plus. I've wolfed down whole packets of ginger nut biscuits, only to lose them to the fishes later on. Acupuncture a couple of days before a trip used to help, but you can't really take your Chinese acupuncturist on board for a whole season.

No, the only one that really works for me is The Patch (Scopolamine). I just stick it under my ear (don't ask me why) and I'm fine.

The ultimate seasickness cure...

And you do get used to the motion eventually. Honest. But if all else fails, there is always the ultimate cure.

22

Getting to the Med

Some would say that getting there is the best bit, and after that they really should have turned right at Cape St Vincent and not left.

There's certainly lots to see along the way, and lots of nautical things to learn even in home waters, such as always making sure you have sufficiently long lines for bow, stern and springs when tying up alongside in tidal areas, like here for example.

Long lines in Portpatrick, Isle of Man

In the Med there's no more than a foot or two of tide, so you won't need to do this. But when the Mistral or the Meltemi try to blow you away for days and days at a time, you'll need your long lines. Sheltering in a bay in Greece, friends on another boat texted us, 'At anchor in bay, 50 knot gusts, 60 metres of anchor chain out, long line tied to a tree.'

The next day they texted, 'At anchor in bay, 60 knot gusts, 60 metres of anchor chain out, long line tied to a tree, second line to a rock.'

They were still there six days later.

Drying out in Truro harbour, Devon

For a yachtie 'drying out' is not always to do with limiting your alcohol consumption. It's also when the tide drains all the water away from your boat, leaving you 'high and dry'. Our first attempt was in Truro alongside the harbour wall (if you can call this typically English day-long 'luvlyweatherfor-ducksahahaha' miserable bloody downpour 'drying out').

But isn't Truro inland? you may ask. Ha! If you time it right the river Fal is navigable all the way up to Truro, and what's more there's a Tesco's right opposite with food and shelter and free newspapers in the café. The Harbourmaster rushed out, amazed that we'd actually been brave (or stupid) enough to enter his harbour, gave us a friendly welcome, then suddenly whipped out his tide tables and peered at them intently. 'Oh. You're OK. Just coming up to springs, you'll get off again tonight about ten. Another day and you'd be here for a fortnight.' Gulp. Another lesson learned.

Of course you'll never need to dry out in the Med because it's not possible without the help of a big crane, but we thought we'd have a go anyway. Just need to develop the technique a bit, that's all.

24

Festival of the Sea,
Brest, Bretagne, France

Crossing the Channel, the weather was kind to us, mainly because we'd waited for it to stop being nasty, and we motored across in a flat calm.

The Festival of the Sea was in its second day. It was by sheer chance we came across it. If you're at all interested in traditional sailing boats, beer, wine, music and dancing, beer, wine, seafood, beer, wine, Breton rare pig breeds, beer, wine, and wooden boat building techniques, you must go.

On the Norwegian stand we glimpsed a craftsman bent over his workbench, apparently engrossed in some intricate joinery work. We hurried over to find a rather well-crafted cheese and tomato sandwich in the making.

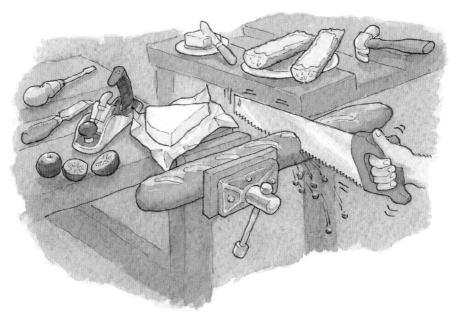

25

A smashing crab restaurant, Brest, Brittany

After the cheese sandwich craftsman, the suspicion that nobody knew how to use a knife and fork in Brest was confirmed for us in a restaurant that served nothing other than huge crabs. Our waitress (not the bald bloke in the picture) brought us each a small plank, a large wooden mallet and a selection of stainless steel devices straight out of a lock picker's tool bag. We were then introduced to the finer points of Breton crab-devouring techniques.

If you wanted a quiet table for a romantic candle-lit dinner for two, this was not the place to be.

The Raz de Seine waypoint, Brittany

But enough of wine, women and crabs; back to the sailing.

There's a rock at the southern end of the Raz de Seine that everyone uses as a waypoint. What's a waypoint? It's an imaginary point on the sea, with a fixed position, that you aim for as you make your way around the coast. It helps you avoid all the hard bits (land, piers, rocks, sand bars, fish farms, oil platforms) which will hurt your boat and give you grief.

The Raz is a tidal race, which can give you a bit of a roller coaster ride. To go through when it's well-behaved, you have to choose your time carefully, and whichever way you approach this waypoint, from North or South, you seem to get there at the same time as everyone else.

On a foggy day of course, you've forgotten all this, and as the fog lifts, you find you're in the nautical equivalent of Piccadilly Circus in the days before Congestion Charges.

And then... the dreaded Bay of Biscay

At this point you wish you'd listened to those people pointing out the charms of the French canal system. We had already crossed Biscay the previous summer in a friend's junk-rigged self-built concrete boat, on a trip complete with engine failure, steering failure, and a buttock-clenching weather forecast you wouldn't want to hear for fear of nerve failure.

When we crossed in Yanina, we motored almost all the way, in a flat calm. Boring but safe. But we were still very, very glad to get to Gijon on the north coast of Spain.

Cider in Gijon

Gijon is great. It's like Brittany with chorizo sausage. The locals pronounce it 'Hee-hon' and their favourite tipple is flat cider.

28

Not many people know that under a European ruling they're not allowed CO_2 in this part of Spain because they keep inhaling it from balloons and talking in squeaky voices. It's a good trick because everybody else has to use helium. Anyway. They've developed this technique to get fizzy cider and it seems to work. The bars all put huge amounts of sawdust on the floor to cope with this, but it does get awfully soggy at the end of an evening.

However, one enterprising bar owner, who was a joiner before he ran a bar, discovered that the sawdust, when compressed, makes a superior form of chipboard (something to do with the alcohol and the absence of CO_2. So he's making big money collecting it from his competitors, who are only too happy to get rid of it, and recycling it to the local chipboard manufacturer who sells the boards on to a well-known furniture retailer to make cider-flavoured drinks cabinets.

None of this is remotely true of course but it's a nice thought.

Legless in the Rias

When we bought Yanina she came with a great pair of legs.

As the tide drops you bolt them on each side and wait till you hit bottom, and if you're lucky you stay upright.

The rias of Northern Spain, still very much tidal, looked like a good opportunity to try them out. You'll never, ever, need to do this in the Med, but what the heck? We had to have a go. We knew we wouldn't be in the Med for ever, and you can't set off round the world with a pair of legs on board and not have a go, can you?

There's a town at the head of one of the rias that you can sail up to on a high tide, bolt your legs on, touch down, and then off you go in your wellies for a coffee and a stroll into town before the sea comes back in again.

But since Prudence is my middle name (my parents went through a very confused stage when I was born), the day before our attempt we decided to take the dinghy up river as the tide fell, looking for spots with a firm bottom.

Ironically, in my youth I was always looking for firm bottoms, but only got the ones with spots. But that's another story.

All excited, we prepared the dinghy for a long trip, spares, fuel, repair kit, grapnel anchor, cheese and pickle sandwiches, lashings of ginger beer and all that sort of thing. Liz was quoting bits from Arthur Ransome and I was feeling like one of the Famous Five, as we set off on the outgoing tide to explore the little-known upper reaches of whatever river it was, so we could see this town I can't remember the name of. This is what we found upriver.

The legs stayed strapped down on deck and have been there ever since. But one day, one day...

To the Algarve...and beyond!

The rias of northern Spain are actually great places to sail and explore and you could spend a lot of time there. Some people stay quite a while.

And then on the way south there are lots of places to stop, like the Islas de Seis, Baiona, and then Lisbon, you can't miss that.

But most yachties are like lemmings. By this I don't mean they're small and furry with suicidal tendencies, but once they've decided on the Med, there's a powerful, determined, unstoppable herd instinct to get to Cape St Vincent (see Route Map, page 110), turn left and head for Gibraltar.

The Algarve coast

Once you *do* round the Cape, you understand the term 'sea change'. After a damp foggy overnight passage accompanied by the ever-present Atlantic swell and the ever-present unlit fishing boats, the Algarve coast gave us sunshine, sparkling seas, and a perfect sail to Lagos Marina, the only one I know where they lift a footbridge to let you in.

The girl on reception looked at her computer screen, then gave us a cheerful smile.

'Welcome back.'

'But we've never been here before.'

'Well, your boat has.'

She's been round the bay a few times, has Yanina.

Further east along the coast there are wild estuaries and lagoons providing safe overnight anchorages, provided you don't forget your tidal range, and provided you don't mind the unlit customs boats lurking around at night, checking your potential for carrying two dozen illegal immigrants in your bilge.

Cadiz

Once you pass the Guadiana river you're in Spain; the river forms the border with Portugal for quite some way inland. However, don't pass it, it's wonderful. There are yachties who got up there and never left, but then that seems to happen all over the Med too. If you do manage to get down again and turn left, stop in Cadiz, a city you can cycle round in a day, full of character and characters, like the snail seller in the old market.

The snail seller in Cadiz market

At last the Med?

Well, *almost.*

But you see once you've got Cadiz under your belt, you're nearly at Gibraltar, guardian of the legendary gateway, the defining point of entry to the Mediterranean, one of the pillars of Hercules, last strategic bastion of the British Empire and the only place along this coast to get a decent English breakfast…

OK, I won't go on about it. It's just that round about here is where you get your first taste of Mediterranean sailing. Here's an extract from our log:

Have you spotted it yet?

That's right.

No frigging wind in the rigging. And when there *is* some it's too much. And then where does it blow?

On the nose. Welcome to sailing in the Med.

Have you considered the merits of a large powerful motorboat?

No?

Well, OK then, you're just as daft as we were. You do have a choice of course. You could always tack upwind to your next port of call, but then you won't get there before dusk, or maybe even a week on Thursday, and by that time you'll certainly have had enough of the Med's short sharp splashy seas. So just carry on motoring into that headwind and the bouncy bits of sea and you'll get there in the end.

But since you still cherish a desire to pull big lumps of cloth around with long bits of string, then it's probably as good a time as any, before we arrive at Gibraltar, to give you ... ***the low-down about the wind situation in the Med.*** Now read on.

The Low-down About The Wind Situation in the Med

Well, I did say didn't I?

If you read other books on sailing in the Med, with titles like 'My Mediterranean Cruising Dream', or 'By Angel's Breath to the Islands' or 'In the Wake of Odysseus', you'll be told that there is a plethora (lots) of winds in the Med, each one with a name and a character and a direction, a time when it blows strongest, whether it's hot or cold or brings red dust with it that turns your deck and fenders pink, and so on and so forth. This is all in fact a total fabrication, a load of hot air, you might say.

I can now reveal that it's all actually a marketing ploy on the part of the little-known Pan-Mediterranean Turistico Organizacione Marinara Internationale di Marketing Européenne, a very low-profile organisation reputed to be clandestinely supported by European funds. You can work out an acronym for yourself.

Its mission is to promote the myth of fabulous endless perfect Mediterranean sailing, wherever you want to go. I mean, with so many winds to choose from how can you go wrong?

Well, let me tell you now, there are in fact only three winds in the entire Mediterranean. Here they are with their officially approved names and English translations:

1	Surlenez	(On the nose)
2	Intrafundamentale	(Up the chuff)
3	Nofuchinaventi	(Buggerall)

These winds are the creation of Pan Med Wind Gods, a consortium which bought out Aeolus (who of course ran the original celestial wind supply monopoly) when he lost his puff (too many Greek cigs) and he couldn't hack it any more.

PMWG then set about a modernisation and cost reduction programme, rationalising the old Mediterranean winds, until each one was replaced by one of the three described above.

With the help of a massive European grant, PMWG developed a radical new form of wind technology called the 'Ventomatico' Wind Synthesiser. With this device one semi-skilled Wind God can control the airflow system over the entire Mediterranean Sea, with nobody any the wiser. Smart eh? The accountants love it.

37

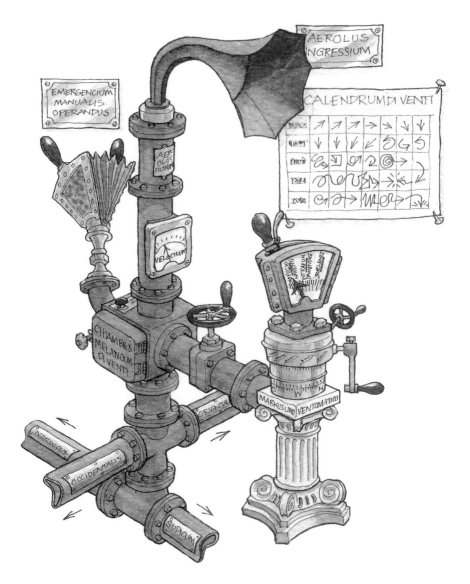

The 'Ventomatico' Wind Synthesiser

Illustration from the Ventomatico Mark 1 Wind Synthesiser Work-shop Manual, discovered behind the shelves of 'Buy and Sell', a unique and fascinating chandlery in Almerimar marina, Spain (see page 52).

Despite the obvious disadvantages to visiting yachtsmen (it doesn't matter a flying fig to the locals, they're all in powerboats), the powers-that-be really had no choice but to fund the project as PMWG threatened to import cheaper, less reliable, foreign winds, mainly from the Far East, such as Hurricanes, Typhoons, and Willy-Willies, with possibly disastrous results.

Hence the situation today where just three synthetic winds have been successfully sold to the entire European, indeed, world yachting market as two or three dozen exotic breezes with classical pedigrees and fancy names. All by a simple marketing 'puff'.

It was sheer commercial genius of course to licence the old names to the motor industry, forever wondering what to call their latest sports cars. A nice little earner. Aeolus eat your heart out. But I digress.

Gibraltar

And so to Gibraltar, the place where, despite its independence, the British Empire still seems to hang on by its fingernails. The place where Johnny Foreigner can see what 'being British' is all about. Where British hospitality and gastronomy rule. Where British holidaymakers can travel to a foreign country without all the tedium of actually meeting any foreigners or eating their food.

To make us really welcome, Gibraltar laid on some fairly thick fog, adding an extra piquancy to the game of Chicken we were playing with the TransMediterraneo ferries.

When eventually we made it to the marina, that night our bottle returned and we just had to celebrate with an impromptu Gibraltar Blues.

We never did find out what the audience on the other boats thought of it, as nobody would speak to us the next day. We left Gibraltar quietly.

Overwintering

It's late September and we really should be... in Tunisia? Well, that's what our original passage plan had said. But here we were still heading east, off the Andalucian coast and motoring in a light swell, diesel fumes wafting into the cockpit from the merest whisper of an Intrafundamentale, or maybe it was just a Nofuchinaventi. Three days later, there we were still heading east, off the Andalucian coast, motoring in a light swell, diesel fumes wafting, etc, etc. You get the picture.

Back in Pwllheli Marina (how long ago was that?) we had met a couple starting their own adventure, who were making for 'that there El Marimar.' Almerimar was our next stop, ideal to leave the boat, hire a car and go to see Granada. We stopped. Three days at the most, we thought. We saw Granada. We came back. And we stayed. In a big sheltered marina with apartments, bars, restaurants, supermarket, cheap flights home, the driest sunniest climate and the cheapest fees in the Western Med.

Tunisia? Sod Tunisia, get the bikes out.

This of course was our first winter on board, and we didn't know what to expect. What do people *do* all winter? For six whole months?

Well… it's a chance to install vital communications equipment…

Essential winter sailing gear

…or purchase essential winter sailing gear...

...or catch up on domestic chores.

One yachtie's rubbish is another's recycling opportunity

On any boat, continued maintenance is vital, and the marina is a reliable source of up-to-date spare parts at very reasonable prices.

You may decide to get off the boat and spend some time in an apartment.

This may be a dangerous move, as it can remind you that there are certain life experiences that living aboard may not provide.

And before you know it...

Quite a few cruising couples decide that they need a change, and decide to sell the boat. There are often a number of highly reputable yacht brokers in the marina only too willing to arrange a sale.

Of course the next step is to buy an apartment. I wrote a song about it to the tune of:

And here it is...

Brown
trousers

I am a salty old skipper.
When I sailed me boat across the Bay of Biscay
It was a rough hairy passage,
Had to wear me brown trousers all the way.

My brown trousers (all sing) My brown trousers

Hairy passage (all sing) Hairy passage

I am a trusty crewmember,
An' I cook an' wash up for that crusty
old bastard I have to call skipper.
I've thrown up more on this trip than I did
when I was carryin' our eldest nipper.

Trusty crew member (all sing) Trusty crew member

Crusty old bastard (all sing) Crusty old bastard

Now we've got an apartment, now we don't have to go to sea no more,
Got a kitchen and bathroom, got full double glazin', an' that ain't all,
When I lean out me window, an' I look over me balcony rail,
I see all you poor buggers, rollin' round in the mother of all gales.

My apartment (all sing) My apartment
Double glazin' (all sing) Double glazin'
You poor buggers! (all sing) You poor buggers!

Making ends meet

But let's assume you resist the temptations of a proper kitchen and bathroom and double glazing, and you're still on board. What can you do to make a few extra bob over the winter?

Most yachties are on a limited budget, and the winter is a chance to top up your cruising funds. Some people go back home and get a job. Some people must be stark staring bonkers. But if that's the only way…

Others have a special skill that's useful to other yachties. I don't have more skills than the average yachtie, not really. I could do you a nice drawing of your fridge but I couldn't mend it for you.

So one way we make a crust is through Liz's design work. On board we have drawing and model-making equipment and an A3 parallel motion drawing board (yes, in a Warrior 35!). We also have 3D CAD software but frankly it's quicker by hand. Liz can sketch ideas, make scale models out of card and aluminium kebab sticks, photograph them, and create presentation pages on the computer ready to email to her clients.

Christmas cards

In our first winter, we made Christmas cards and sold them on the Sunday morning market. We sold enough to pay for the week's groceries, but on a bright Sunday morning the real fun was meeting all the people we'd been getting plastered with the night before. Here are some cards:

By December the marina was almost full.

The marina's population of small dogs and cats, none of whom seemed to belong to anyone, roamed around at will, and it was up to you to avoid the evidence of their wanderings. But around Christmas, there was evidence of a different kind.

And if you're Father Christmas, how do you get presents to people living on boats? Rudolph thought he knew how.

The Christmas cards led to commissions

Jane and her husband Gard run a second-hand chandlery shop in the marina, where stock control and retrieval was always a major issue for them. I designed this handy piece of equipment to enable them to reach all the items on their shelves in a matter of seconds.

When I first put the proposal to them and showed them this drawing, they were so overwhelmed by a design solution of such breathtaking and elegant simplicity that they just stared at me, mouths open, and didn't say anything for a good while. I think they were a bit in awe to be honest.

Music

I've mentioned musicians already. Pat, seen here looking through the window, was better described as an aging muso. That's how somebody described me once but Pat's *much* more eligible for the title. He was in a band in the '60s, he knows all the right people in the music business, he once owned a pair of crocodile skin cowboy boots, and by ten o'clock every night you'll find him floating round the ceiling in a cloud of smoke. Man.

Pat was enterprising enough to organise a jam session in a bar, all musicians invited. Of course, about 150 yachties, starved of entertainment, arrived too. The bar made record profits that night, a band was born, and Pat had spawned a monster.

We played a few more evenings, gradually adding more songs to the repertoire, until on the New Year's Eve gig we actually got paid in euros and not just beer. Maybe I shouldn't admit that, my accountant might read this.

It's Spring!

We might even go sailing...

Do you remember that TV series 'The Prisoner' with Patrick McGoohan? Every time he tried to escape from that charming Italianate village in North Wales he'd get chased along the beach by a giant bouncing rubber ball? No, neither do I. I'm too young. But then I also lie about my age.

And stuck in the marina in blustery April, with day after day of easterly gales, with 3 or 4 metre waves 'out there', with the wind gusting up to 70 knots (that's a hurricane, I reckon, so thanks a bundle, Pan Med Wind Gods), every yachtie feels that if the weather doesn't stop misbehaving and give us a few days of westerlies so we can get up the coast and across to Ibiza and get our kit off in the sunshine, then like Patrick McGoohan, we'll *never* leave. We'll all be in apartments and running laundrettes with signs on the washing machines saying 'Do not wash rope in this machine.' Unlike Patrick McGoohan. I don't think he ever ran a laundrette.

Yachties are huddled together in the internet café, checking a dozen weather websites. Wind speed and direction, wave heights, swell, barometric pressure and humidity are all weighed and considered. Back on board, wind-flayed sunburnt ears bend to the SSB radio, trying to make out predictions from Monaco (receiving an SSB broadcast is like listening

to a dalek through a cocoa tin on a piece of string). GRIB files (raw computer data untouched by Michael Fish) are down-loaded onto laptops; weather texts are received on mobile phones. Somebody checks the Daily Mail weather page. It says 'Madrid: sunny.' Gnarled fingers are traced across the Coptic Storm Calendar's predictions (see Rod Heikell's 'Mediterranean Cruising Handbook').

Some marinas even have weather stones hanging up outside. If the stone is dry, it's not raining; if it's wet, it is. If it's warm the sun's out. If it's moving... you get the idea.

Eventually, some intrepid madman disconnects his Sky TV dish and sticks a 'For Sale' sign on it, unplugs his shore power, winds up his water hose, slips his lines and heads off into the vast expanse of the ocean, the great blue unknown, to who knows which exotic destination, Menorca or Morocco, Venice or Venezuela, Garrucha or Grimsby.

Our neighbours, an American couple, were busy preparing to leave.

'Where to? Ibiza? Sardinia? Italy?' I asked.

In true Buzz Lightyear style, the response was: 'To Roquetas… and beyond!'

Roquetas was five miles up the coast.

But here's a tip for when you *do* decide to go, particularly if you are bows-to in your berth (in layman's terms: if your backside is sticking out from the concrete bit) *and* you've been greedy and used two lazy lines. Don't do what we did and put the engine into gear before the lines had dropped clear of the prop.

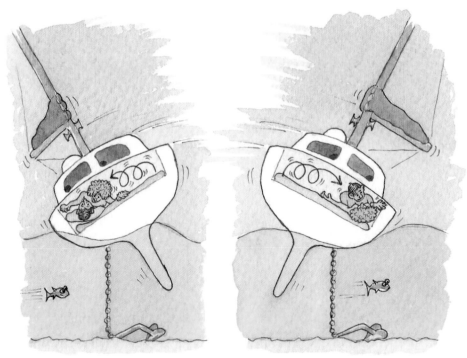

Togetherness is a rolly anchorage

And then you're out of the marina. After months of enforced idleness, your boat surges forward, its sails snapping in the wind, eagerly thrusting through a sparkling sea. The sun glints cheerfully on your bald patch and the breeze teasingly runs its fingers through whatever hair you have left up there.

You've had a great day's sail, you're ready to spend your first night at anchor, and you remember all about the gentle movement of the waves rocking you to sleep, and the feeling of safety and security engendered by hanging onto a rusty chain attached to a convoluted lump of metal resting on the seabed.

So before we go off sailing to exotic places and start enjoying ourselves, let's have a look at the gentle but crucial art of anchoring in the Med.

Anchoring in the Mediterranean

Like anywhere else, the Med's bottom is sand, mud or rock. But there's lots of dense weed, except in small harbours where it's just nasty thick evil-smelling turgid grey-brown ooze into which no self-respecting weed will poke its roots. So your anchor will have to do a lot of gardening. Get one with a nice sharp point.

And of course the best winds for sailing occur when you're at anchor, courtesy of our friends the Pan Mediterranean Wind Gods. Apparently if they don't use up all the wind each day, they have to release it overnight, otherwise there's a surplus which gets all mixed up with the next day's wind, and the next, until it all goes horribly wrong.

Here in Torrevieja harbour at 7 in the morning an incompetent trainee Wind God, just starting his shift, accidentally flipped a gentle Surlenez into a lively Intrafundamentale, and three or four boats drifted downwind towards us, dislodged anchors bouncing along the seabed. One boat came too close for comfort, both ours and the unfortunate skipper's.

Anchoring techniques can vary considerably

It seems to me there are definite national characteristics when it comes to anchoring techniques.

Being British, we put our chain out to four times the depth, check our turning circle for the tide, do the Tom Cunliffe 'nibble-and-bite' technique to dig the hook well in, and then go below for a well-earned cuppa and a Jaffa cake, secure in the knowledge of a job well done.

Then some Frenchman comes along, drops his anchor straight on top of ours, shrugs gallically as only a Frenchman can, jumps into his dinghy and zips ashore for some snails and a glass of Pernod. I mean it's just not on, is it?

There are some Italians who adopt a very similar approach but with the difference that their anchor will have been liberated from someone else's boat.

Along with the fenders. The dinghy. The outboard. The odd winch or two. Maybe the wind generator, depends whether they've lifted any spanners or not.

In crowded anchorages in the Balearics, Spanish sailors often like to show off by silently sailing, engine off, through all the narrowest gaps, finally settling on a spot about two yards from your pulpit, so that when they *do* drag anchor at 4am, they'll score a direct hit, bend a stanchion or two then run around acting all surprised about it.

Whereas some German sailors like to demonstrate their innate thoroughness and competence by putting out a thoroughly competent amount of chain, and informing any others within hailing distance of that fact, thus ensuring nobody gets too close.

This of course is all part of the game of Anchor Man's Bluff that we all play.

Persistence to the point of...

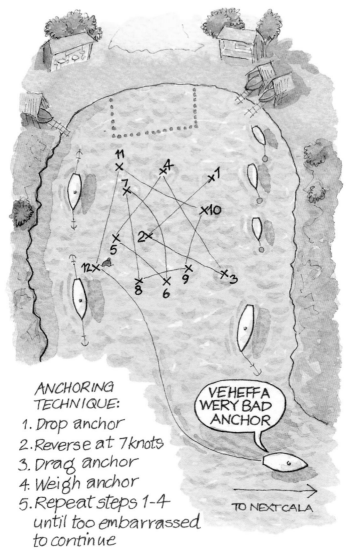

Some skippers think that you need 5000 revs in reverse to set an anchor. In a cala in Ibiza where we'd been anchored for a few days, we watched from the beach as a boat zoomed back and forth, trying to dig the anchor in.

...desperation

We packed our beach stuff up, rowed the dinghy back to Yanina, and they were still trying, half way through attempt number 11. Finally a mooring buoy looked like the answer. One of the crew leapt into the water and tied onto it, then swam to attention awaiting further orders.

Attempt Nº 12

Presumably he would be despatched over the side the next morning to untie it. Or maybe they would just leave him there, you never know.

It was an unorthodox technique but I thought it deserved full marks for determination. But the skipper pulled a face. They were too close to us. As we handed them their dinghy oar which Liz had rescued, the skipper said sadly:

'Ve vill go to the next cala, ve have a very bad anchor.'

It was a CQR just like ours.

Our feeling of self-righteous smugness lasted until that night when we set off for an overnight passage to Majorca in the pitch black, got the mainsail jammed halfway up the mast, shouted a lot at each other, and limped back into the cala, spotting the rocks by torchlight, until we could re-anchor. But only once.

Trying not to go aground

When you get the kind of weather we got in Ajaccio, Corsica, it just doesn't matter how well your anchor is set. You lose the plot completely, and all that smugness from watching other people's anchoring techniques evaporates as 45 knots of wind flips your hook out of its little toehold behind a small rock on the seabed. Experienced skippers went into panic mode, hanging on to anything their boat is drifting past. One athletic type jumped onto a ferry-mooring buoy only to be dragged off again. Another grabbed Liz's hand on his way downwind. She shook it politely before gently releasing it, saying, 'So long and watch out for that jetty over there.'

The key phrase to listen out for on the weather forecast is 'Forts raffalés'. And then in half an hour it's all over.

Going aground

And if the worst does happen and you go aground, there's often help at hand. In Elba, we left Yanina at anchor and went off on a bus. The wind changed and the anchor decided to take a walk.

We returned to find Yanina swaying gently the wrong side of a marker buoy, grinding her keel between a couple of rocks. We spent the night grinding our teeth and listening to it, imagining huge chunks of lead and fibreglass bouncing off the seabed.

In the morning, the local safety bloke arrived, his RIB curving to a stop in a wall of spray. He and his rather glamorous girlfriend (black wet-suits always do it for me; it's the combination of rubber and zips I think) turned their Ray-Bans on us and dazzled us with smiles a foot wide.

Behind them a shiny black outboard motor the size of a small shed throbbed and burbled to itself, waiting for the chance to show off. Within minutes a line was round our mast, the outboard roared, and we were dragged off sideways to safe water.

Sailing

in the

Yes, despite being British we all do it. We may not do it with the thoroughness of the Germans, the panache of the French, or the abandon of the Italians, but in a secluded anchorage where you won't frighten the neighbours, in a sunny 35 degrees, and in 4 or 5 metres of lovely clear warm salty water just a wild leap, or for the more cautious, a swim ladder away, well, it'd be rude not to be nude.

So gradually you get comfortable with the idea of wandering about the boat with no kit on, sleeping, reading, eating, even cooking (an apron is a good idea though, particularly if you're frying eggs), and you begin to relish the great feeling of freedom that it engenders. So why stick to the secluded anchorage to indulge?

Even in a crowded harbour, if you've got a deep centre cockpit and spray dodgers like us, you can get your all-over tan in peace… usually.

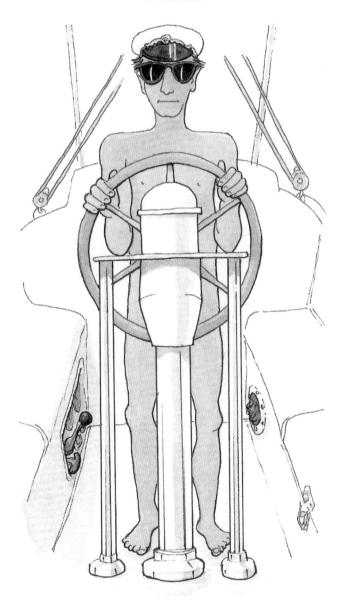

And although you've swapped your sailor suit for your birthday suit, you can still cut a dash at the helm.

The French, the Italians, the Spanish, indeed the Germans, the Dutch, the Scandinavians, and for all I know the whole of New Europe, seem to handle luffing in the buff with nonchalance, ease and a complete lack of embarrassment.

But it's often the British single-hander, who has been away from polite society for far too long, who fails to observe the finer points of nude sailing etiquette. Unfortunately, his neighbours can't fail to observe *his* finer points.

Guests on board

Despite the fridge, the telly, hot water out of the tap, microwave ovens, washing machines, crocheted cushion covers (and sometimes crocheted winch covers) and all the other home comforts some yachties manage to get on board, they are still on a boat, and the life and values are quite different from those on land.

It's difficult to get this over to guests who haven't sailed before. 'How many suitcases can I bring?', 'Will we go out of sight of land?', 'So you're in Greece, can you meet me in Barcelona next Thursday?'

A comfortable day's journey for a pair of liveaboards can be anything from 10 to 50 miles; that's an hour up the motorway at the most for everyone else. So meeting up is the first problem to overcome, and it can either mean you use up 200 quid's worth of fuel motoring across half the Med to meet someone who's booked a flight that cost a tenner, or on the other hand, staying in one spot for two months checking the weather forecasts to make sure you'll actually be where you said you would be when you all agreed it would be 'lovely to meet up'.

So, like many others living on board we have now made it a rule that 'they come to us, we don't go to them'.

And once your guests have managed to find you, and are looking forward to their first experience of life on board, it's wise to guide them through the boat's little idiosyncrasies, such as the fact that your water comes from a couple of tanks under the floor and not from a reservoir in North Wales. Indeed, conserving water is a major issue, unless of course you've spent a few grand on a water maker, a remarkable but expensive device which converts sea water to fresh. Saves on tank storage but you can buy a couple of years' supply of Perrier for about the same outlay.

You can always spot a yachtie with a water maker. They're out hosing the salt off their decks and sails in some remote anchorage miles from the nearest quayside tap, while we make do with a couple of Wet Wipes.

Anyway, here's a great way to shower and save water. Get yourself a small plastic washing-up bowl, and follow the instructions in this drawing. Even better, stand in it, catch as much water as you can, then put it in the toilet seat, and bingo! You have a bidet. How many boats have got that?

And now that you've seen a drawing of our bathroom (oh alright, the heads, if you're going to be all salty about it), we can discuss that most fundamental piece of boat equipment which, for all those new to boats, will be an intriguing and delightful surprise.

And if not, it'll be the cause of a week or so's panic attacks and nervous constipation.

Illustration based on 'The Scream' by Edvard Munch. Keep taking the tablets, Edvard.

The marine toilet

Ignoring for now the high tech luxury push button thrones, there are basically three types of marine toilet, fundamentally important because two of them are capable of sinking the boat if they go wrong (they're connected to holes in the bottom of the boat), and the third is very useful to prevent such an occurrence.

sit here after
lifting lid

seal

seal!

The vacuum toilet

Number 1: The Vacuum Toilet

As its name suggests it works by vacuum. You put the lid down on the seat and a rubber seal stops the air getting in. You pump away and seawater is drawn in, through, and out, flushing it. Dead simple, and very reliable. They last forever. Very important though, particularly if you have a big bottom that could create an airtight seal on the seat, not to start pumping while still seated. Your piles might start to throb uncomfortably, and much worse, you might never, ever, get off.

The solution here is to either sit there until you lose enough weight to make your bottom a bit bonier, or get a (very good) friend to slide a well-greased long slim object like a ruler (don't ever let them use a bread knife) between you and the seat, thus breaking the seal and allowing you instant relief for your piles.

Number 2: The Pump Toilet

This is the one we've got. It has a sort of big bike pump on the side with a little lever on top. Flick it left and you pump sea water in on the up stroke and out on the down stroke, flick it right and you just pump it all out, flushed with success, as they say. Again, simple and pretty reliable.

However, if you, you know, go off in a dream, or just forget, or get it all wrong and just keep pumping with said lever on the right, with no more water coming in, you can create an interesting phenomenon we call 'blowback'. We've seen this only once. Once was enough.

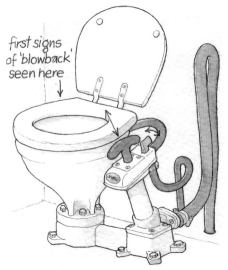

first signs of 'blowback' seen here

The pump toilet

Number 3: The Bucket

Not connected to any holes in the bottom of the boat, and in terms of containers to be found on board, ideal (better than, say, a saucepan, and *much* better than a colander) for the 'bucket-and-chuck-it' method.

Also the preferred equipment for most round-the-world racing yachtsmen. They of course tend to use Teflon-lined buckets transfer-injection-moulded in an epoxy-Kevlar matrix with pre-stressed carbon fibre handles, for performance performing, as it were.

But for most of us the ubiquitous builder's bucket would suffice if your guest is still vacuum-sealed onto the seat, or busy cleaning up the blowback.

sit here

The ubiquitous builder's bucket

72

Places & people

I don't want this book to be a travelogue, but all I've told you about so far are toilets, naked sailors and anchoring techniques. You could be anywhere. As Mae West once said, 'I've been things and seen places,' so in that spirit here are a few sights, people, places and thoughts on the Mediterranean experience.

You may feel chronologically challenged at this point, because we set off in the spring, took our clothes off in the summer, and yet now we're going to dodge back to Christmas in Andalucia and then work our way to September in Sicily.

Bear with me, dear reader, it will be worth it.

Really...

Christmas in Andalucía

Nothing much happens in Spain on Christmas Day. It's a holiday, but there's no mad scramble to tear wrapping paper off prezzies. Spanish parents realised long ago that if Santa's got to make his way down from Lapland, climb down chimneys everywhere from Basingstoke to Basel, run out of presents, go back for more, get fresh supplies of reindeer nuts, they'll be lucky to see him in Andalucía much before Easter. And you couldn't expect the little baby Jesus to come up with the goods on the night before Christmas, the kid wasn't even born then.

boiled sweets

And so the Spanish celebrate on the 6th of January with the Three Kings. Kings, you will note, not Three Wise Men. We all know that academic achievement is not the quickest way to get rich, but a King? Well, he's *born* with it isn't he, because his dad and his granddad and his great-granddad robbed all of his subjects of their pennies a long way back. That's what the Spanish thought anyway.

And according to reliable Spanish records, it was the 6th when the Three Kings arrived. A bit late for most of us maybe, but at least they were spared the whole birth in the stable bit, with Joseph and Mary in the middle of a domestic (Joseph: 'So who was it then? And don't give me all that about God again, do you think I was born yesterday?'). And Jesus would have been a bit more presentable by that time - clean set of swaddling clothes, halo just beginning to glow, smile just starting to get beatific, and so on.

On the big day we were in a town up in the hills above Malaga, watching a procession of flat top lorries with floats grinding their stop-start way up the hill to the Plaça Major amid a nose-tingling aroma of burning clutch.

The first carried papier-mâché statues of the Kings. The next few were presumably the Kings' retinue and hangers-on, and on each lorry, literally hanging on was a gaggle of local children, flinging sweets into the crowd as they passed. Not your soft marshmallows or choccies but those hard boiled sweets in cellophane wrappers, the kind that take ages to suck, and really sting when they hit your ear.

Enterprising children in the crowd, racing around scrabbling for sweets, had also planted elderly relatives as 'sweepers'. Just as you, a foreign gringo, bent down to pick up a couple of sweets, a walking stick would dart between your legs, deftly flick the sweets away, and then deliver a smart tap to the shin.

One of the last lorries rolled to a stop in front of us. A dozen diminutive Santas were seated on the flat top, bored and fed up with giving away all their sweets. The driver, clearly anxious to get home to a slice of ham and a vaso de tinto, let in the clutch just a little too impatiently, and as the lorry lurched forward, so half a dozen bored little Santas rolled rapidly off the back, bored no more.

So forget frankincense and myrrh, or even the latest PlayStation. As gifts from afar these Kings brought boiled sweets.

Brian on Spaceship

Brian was a fascinating character. Having previously owned every kind of boat from a Chinese junk to a home-made hovercraft, he had now retired to live on board in one of the many marinas in Southern Spain. Quite a few yachties live in marinas permanently. But they are on boats that were built to cross oceans. That's a lot of redundant features that never get to be used as they were intended.

Brian's genius was in recognising this. His aim was 'maximum luxury in minimum space'. Throwing away the yacht designer's rulebook, along with a lot of the things that make a boat look like a boat, he produced the remarkable 'Spaceship'. An elegant and refined cruiser it is not. Practical and fit for his purpose it certainly is.

Fitting in the smallest and cheapest marina slot at just under 8 metres, yet it has a king size double bed, a bathroom with a shower and hot water tank, a kitchen with full size washer-dryer, domestic cooker and sink unit, a plasma TV screen viewed from a leather swivel armchair, and enough headroom for a six-footer like Brian.

No water tanks in the bilge. No bilge. Just fix the hose onto the pontoon tap. No big diesel engine, no fuel tank, just a modest outboard motor. No set of hefty 12 volt batteries, just plug into shore power.

'Spain's not cheap any more these days,' said Brian the last time we saw him. He looked longingly out to sea. 'Now Morocco's over there, an' it's only 50 miles. They've got some cheap marinas there, tha' knows.'

The cave houses of Galera

If you take the motorway from Almeria to Granada, round the back of the Alpujarra hills, you can stop at a small town called Galera. The hillsides around it are soft sandstone, and they're peppered with caves. The stone is so soft you can almost dig it out with your fingernails. So Galera's suburbs, on three sides at least, are all cave houses. They're dry, comfortable, temperature-controlled, and if you want a second bathroom or a loft conversion, well, you just dig one out. A lot are unused or derelict, but a local entrepreneur has bought a large number and turned them into just the sort of smart residence that you might buy if you were bored with your villa in Tuscany. So now even the most improbable hole scooped out of the hillside has a 'For Sale' sign up.

We go to the dogs

With some friends we spent a week house-sitting in a three-bedroom cave house above Galera. This actually meant a week looking after four dogs and two cats for the absent owner. The cats looked after themselves, as cats do, but as for the dogs, just look at this lot:

Sophie with the mad eyes, who growled to herself constantly while fixing a baleful glare onto you.

Pale brown eyes

Black

Sophie

'Brain' on forehead

Bald tail

Brains

Brains, so unbelievably ancient that he just about managed to totter from bed to food bowl and back again. Brains was not his real name but we decided that the unfortunate growth on his forehead, just where his third eye might have been, was where his brain had migrated to the outside of his skull.

Jamie was the most dull, thick, moronic animal I think I will ever come across, but then I'm always meeting new people so I could be wrong...

Jamie

Rastus with the bat ears

But Rastus with the big bat ears was a delight. Liz wanted to kidnap him and take him back to the boat.

Seville and Cordoba

If you carry on along the road from Galera and don't turn into a lay-by, you'll get to Granada, and then Cordoba and Seville, and you'll definitely turn into a tourist. We had the chance of going to Seville in Easter Week, when there are 52 holy processions in seven days, each with their own Virgin Mary at its head, followed by the hooded penitents of 52 different Brotherhoods, each pointy-hooded brother carrying a four-foot long lighted candle. You can't help expecting Ku Klux Klan members to turn up carrying shotguns instead of candles.

For an incredibly detailed description of Semana Santa, read 'On the Shores of the Mediterranean' by Eric Newby, who actually took part in it and wrote an exhaustive account of the whole thing. And all week long there's nowhere at all to stay. All full up.

So we went the week before. Having read Newby's book and cross-referenced it with our well-thumbed 'Rough Guide', neither of us could face the scourgings, the crucifixions, the pain and the pointy hoods. But we did get a room, and we did see Seville, and we're very glad that we did.

So all I can offer is this soft cuddly penitente I saw in a shop window in Cordoba, who looks as if he's not really into scourging, more likely the soft cushion torture that Monty Python's Spanish inquisitors used to favour. Perhaps he's a Cordoban comment on their fanatical neighbours in Seville.

Cuddly penitente with candle

Ibiza drumfest

Sail east from mainland Spain to Ibiza, and you couldn't have a greater contrast. Instead of all the Virgin Mary fanatics in robes and pointy hoods, there are sun-worshippers in nothing but a pair of flip-flops.

And there's definitely no scourging. Incense burners and four-foot candles are replaced by cannabis fumes and conga drums every Sunday night when the hippies gather for their drumfest in Cala Beniras.

Admittedly, some of them are 'Hampstead Hippies', wearing brand new sandals and freshly-laundered kaftans, here to drop out for a week or two's Indian head massage and meditation classes. But then the '60s are long gone, man.

Fine art in Formentera

There's a stony beach at the north end of Formentera that has been turned into an outdoor sculpture gallery. It's all the work of one man. Littered with rocks and stones already carved and scoured into fantastic shapes by sea and wind, the beach is his raw material, his studio, sculpture yard and exhibition space.

He's there some days, in a little stone shelter with a driftwood roof, looking out to sea, while his skeleton, seen here, lies prone but somehow erect.

Mallorca up north

The north west coast of Mallorca.

No high-rise apartments or hotels. No crowded beaches. No British pubs or Irish bars.

Just a rugged mountainous coast-line with safe harbours like Andraitx and Soller, and spectacular anchorages like this one at the Torrente de Pareis...

...and wonderful hill villages like Deya, where Robert Graves lived. The churchyard on top of the hill has views to die for. This is Graves' grave.

Touring Formentor

Carry on sailing up the north west coast until you can turn right, and you're at the Formentor peninsula, the wildest and ruggedest bit of all Mallorca.

If you're *really* keen, or if the sun's fried your brains and you've lost all judgmental skills, you can renew your sense of adventure and throw security to the winds by doing what we did. Just leave the boat at anchor, drop the bikes (in pieces) into the dinghy, leave the dinghy tied to a rock, re-assemble the bikes, and pedal and push your parched, sweaty, aching way up to the lighthouse where there is, fortunately, a café selling simple refreshments, but at prices that would outdo the Savoy Grill.

It's much quicker on the way back, with a swim and a beer to look forward to at the end.

Festa de Sant Joan, Ciudadella, Menorca

There are festivals all over the Med. The ones we read about we always seemed to miss, then others we just stumbled on, like the Festa de Sant Joan (St John to you) in Ciudadella, in the old port.

Walking into town we found the streets full of litter, as if someone had just had a great party. Looking over a wall we saw people drinking, laughing, dancing in the street below. Closer to the port, the crowd thickened until there were thousands more, also laughing and drinking but with no room to dance. Crammed into a flat sandy area at the head of the port, they were a good-natured lot of drunks, at the 'swaying' stage of drunkenness, just before the 'falling over' stage. We pushed our way forward into the constantly moving crowd, amongst which horses and riders posed, allowing people to admire them. On the edges of the crowd were Red Cross tents. The sense of anticipation was turned up as tight as a tourniquet as we saw nurses pulling on surgical gloves, in preparation for - what?

As the horses and riders gathered around a platform, warnings were issued over the loudspeakers in half a dozen languages, asking the crowd to keep clear of the horses, but it was a formality. The crowd just carried on with its business of being a crowd and enjoying itself. The riders were being issued with long wooden lances. A bass drum started to beat, slowly and deliberately, followed by some strange medieval piping, and a horseman suddenly spurred his mount into a gallop, his lance levelled, straight into the densest part of the crowd.

Watching the crowd open up in front of the horse and immediately close again behind it was a bit like watching someone pull a knife through treacle on a plate, except that the horse left a trail of people lying on the ground where they'd toppled over, already at the 'falling over' stage of drunkenness.

As the horse and rider approached their target (we never got to see what it was) the crowd roared, breaking into a cheer as the target was hit. Those still standing jumped up and down. A few more fell over. The drum beat again. Then the piping. Another horse thundered down the same path. People stood up just in time to fall back out of the path of the flying hooves, roaring, cheering and laughing from a horizontal position on the ground.

It all went on for a couple of hours. We found out afterwards that there are serious injuries every year, sometimes fatal. Just a harmless bit of fun, Menorcan style.

In bed that night about midnight I realised that a fireworks display had started. I got up into the cockpit and watched for a good few minutes. 'Come and have a look, Liz.' Liz looked out and said, 'I think *you'd* better have a look - behind you.' I heard ragged applause and raucous laughter as I turned to look back. The phrase 'Nice arse meester' is now firmly implanted into my brain.

Busking in Mahon

This should really be in the 'Making ends meet' section, because on our first try we made 80 euros in under two hours. And we received lots of polite and helpful encouragement from an appreciative and cultured audience.

A Sardinian welcome

Sardinia always used to be known as a mysterious inhospitable sort of island, populated by cut-throats, brigands and bandits. The sort of place that nobody went to and if they did they didn't linger. Read D. H. Lawrence's 'Sea and Sardinia' for an enjoyable bad-tempered rant about the land, the people and the total absence of toilets.

We went there only briefly so I can't tell you if it's changed much since Lawrence's day. However I do know that the Costa Smeralda is probably the most expensive place to park your boat in the Med, so presumably they have toilets now.

Four boats crossed together from Menorca to Sardinia. Three of us arrived and anchored in the bay. Hours later we received a text from the fourth: 'Outside bay engine dead no wind any chance of a tow?' Our friends on Aimee had finally arrived, and we towed them into the anchorage to join the others. We all slept soundly that night.

The next morning three boats were minus their shiny new dinghies and outboard motors (we still had ours; they're too scruffy for the Sardinian Dinghy Liberation Front to bother with).

Welcome to Sardinia, folks.

After staying to ferry others to the bus stop to get to town and make their insurance claims we headed off on our way to Corsica the next day.

It would have been good to see more of Sardinia, but we were on a bit of a mission. We had arranged to meet some friends on the Italian mainland (see page 68 for what we *should* have done), and our last stop in Sardinia was Stintino.

Ice cream in Stintino

Once a fishing village and now a holiday resort for the Italians, Stintino had the benefit of an abandoned marina in its outer harbour. Free moorings! OK, so this is how it works; they take your dinghy and outboard but give you free mooring. Interesting.

The other memorable aspect of Stintino was the Gelateria. The Italians have gelaterias like we have chip shops, and at about ten o'clock at night, instead of calling in after a few pints for a bag of fish and chips with curry sauce and mushy peas, they form a noisy but orderly rabble around the gelateria and demand huge tubs of ice cream in all sorts of colours and flavours.

I tried to do you a drawing of the crowded gelateria, but frankly, it takes a long time to draw all those people (what do you expect at this price, blood?), so I somehow ended up with this. I don't know why, and I can't think of what goes in the speech bubble either.

If you can, email me at nosetheon@yahoo.co.uk, and whoever comes up with the best one will get a copy of the next book.

Corsica. It's so rugged

Of all the islands in the Med that deserve the term 'rugged' the most ruggedest one that outdoes all the others in sheer unadulterated rugged ruggedness, is Corsica. Unless it's Sardinia, but I don't know.

Everywhere you look, from the sea or from the seat of a hire car, the rock that forms Corsica is twisted, tortuous, wild, sharp, jagged, and definitely rugged. And the creatures that you come across are also wild and rugged. Wild boar roam the rugged forests and hills. When we drove up there we met some, wildly lying in the rugged road, waiting to be given a sandwich and have their ears scratched.

The 'wild' boars of Corsica

Italy's thigh

If you see the map of Italy as a giant leg, then Genoa has got to be the crotch. It was certainly hot and sweaty when we were there. And as you might expect, the areas close to the crotch are extremely attractive to tourists, holidaymakers and yachties alike. Well, we're only human... most of us. But as you grope your way down Italy's thigh, the west coast becomes very flat and a bit dull, and gradually less interesting as somewhere to sail (or grope). You have to go to the Tuscan islands and Elba for that (or that).

Let's face it, you're feeling your way down the coast so you can penetrate Pisa, thrust into Tuscany, have a legover in Livorno, and what you do with Florence is your business. And later if you're still not satisfied, you can ravish Ravenna, although you'd have to get a bus over to the east coast to do that.

But while you're still in Pisa, there's one photograph that you just have to take...

So, leaving all smutty innuendo behind us, we perambulated Pisa, flitted round Florence, sauntered through Siena and traversed Tuscany.

But Rome. Rome was our ruin. From the Forum to the Coliseum to St Peter's Square to the Sistine Chapel, it's all so massively, overwhelmingly, hugely, pompously, determined to impress. And because of that you can't take it seriously... well, I can't.

The Grandeur that was Rome...

Rome

Like good tourists we 'did' all the sights, including the Coliseum, complete with genuine centurion and ever-present queue. But queuing in the hot sun was exhausting. Maybe it was time to head indoors.

According to our guide, entry to the Sistine Chapel was free on the last Sunday of each month, which was by sheer good luck, the next day.

Sorted! But a few thousand others had read the same guide and got there ahead of us, and so we joined an even bigger queue in the hot sun.

91

Four hours later we were shuffling with the crowd through endless corridors stuffed with Vatican treasures, on our way to see Michelangelo's ceiling. There was some stunning stuff to shuffle past; acres and acres of ancient painted canvas, tons and more tons of exquisitely sculpted marble.

Each piece deserved at least five minutes of contemplation. But you couldn't stop shuffling for a moment because of the shufflers behind you. We shuffled on. We shuffled in. The Chapel was filled with other shufflers craning their necks and squinting their eyes trying to make sense of Michelangelo's brushstrokes 150 feet above their heads.

'So is this what being a tourist is all about? There's got to be a better way,' I muttered to Liz.

'Let me think about it,' she said.

It wasn't till we got a bit further down the coast to Anzio, that we came up with the brainwave that will make our fortune, that the Rome Tourist Board (when you're in Rome, ask for the *Bordello Turistico di Roma*) won't be able to turn down, that will make the royalties from this book look like peanuts. Actually that won't be difficult. Anyway, if you want to go swimming in Anzio, you find that the beach is actually in what was the Emperor Nero's harbour. Just imagine it...

92

Those half-sunken stone breakwaters used to be the harbour wall. Triremes used to tie up there. And those holes in the rock face behind the beach used to be the Harbourmaster's office. What's left of Nero's seaside holiday home overlooks hundreds of happy relaxed tourists, swimming, sunbathing and eating ice cream, all in a major archaeological site. Culture *can* be fun! So what could you do in Rome?

A funny thing swam up to me on my way to the Forum

Why not get a few JCBs in and dig out this linear swimming pool in the Forum? You could float gently past all the cultural bits and bobs the Romans want you to be impressed with, and then maybe stop for a spell on a sunlounger, get the headphones on and grab a bit of historical background info while you top up your tan.

And you wouldn't have to walk all over the place, that's for sure.

This discreet overhead track would whizz you past all the sights in comfort and complete safety without your feet touching the pavement.

The Spanish Steps – our overhead tourist conveyance system would be a speedy and conven-ient way to see the sights in any city...

And it doesn't spoil the view one little bit.

The Sistine Chapel as you've never seen it

And Liz's idea for the Sistine Chapel? Wouldn't take long to knock this up, would it? Then you could see all the cherubim's and seraphim's pink bits in close-up, thrill at the vibrant brushwork, marvel at the baroque intensity of the composition, and wonder what on earth Michelangelo's neck must have felt like by the time he'd finished.

I just hope he could afford a good physio.

Contemporary art in Rome

But just as important as Michelangelo and all his mates is the huge wealth of Roman modern art, from painting…

...to sculpture. And they don't tuck it away in a gallery, they display it right on the streets, as seen here outside this café.

Marvellous stuff.

Aspects of the Italian character

In Italy we've witnessed acts of overwhelming kindness, and on the other hand, opportunistic daylight robbery.

In Genoa, I foolishly put a 20 Euro note into a ticket machine for a funicular tram, for two 75 cent tickets. Too late, I discovered that the machine didn't give change.

On the way up, we chatted to a charming old man, pleased to be able practise his English. At the top we asked the two uniformed tram ticket supremos for our change. 'No! Impossibile!' They wanted us to go to the Uffizi Centrale di Transportazione Genovese to fill in a few forms and get our money back. We were sailing the next day, we tried to explain. Arms were folded. Glares were exchanged. Stalemate.

With courteous civility, our new friend intervened, translating for us and pleading our case with much gesturing but little success. Finally, with the uniforms looking on, he offered to buy the tickets from us.

'No, no, really, it's our fault, you mustn't,' we said.

'But I insist.'

'No, we couldn't possibly.'

Our friend pulled out his wallet with a flourish and waved a handful of notes around.

'I really insist.'

'No, honestly, please.'

It was touching. It was heart-felt. It was a moment of noble self-lessness that transcended national boundaries. You could almost hear the violins.

Uniform Number One, wiping a tear from his cheek, pulled himself together and issued a rapid order to Uniform Number Two to open the cash box. After some form filling we were on our way, with our change in our pockets. And so was our kind old man, with his honour intact.

Here is another example: it was just into September, out of season, further down the coast in Scario harbour, where we met our footballer a few pages on from here. Nobody was about to collect mooring fees and we didn't ask. A German yachtsman tied up alongside a local fishing boat. Scrupulously honest, he asked the fisherman who he should pay. 'You can pay me, signore. That will be 30 euros.' The German paid, only realising he'd been had when he told us about it. He shrugged and put it down to experience.

Early the next morning, the fisherman knocked on his hull. 'For you, signore.' He handed him a large fish, part of his night's catch. 'They'll cook it for you at the ristorante.'

Neapolitan housewives go shopping

Further south and Napoli beckoned to us like a street vendor selling fake watches. Naples' reputation goes before her. Pickpockets! Muggers! Shall we go or shan't we? We did, and we loved it. They still lower their baskets down to the street vendors just like in the old '50s Italian films.

And Naples gave us Sophia Loren, so it's got my vote.

Macho Man in Capri

Outside the Bay of Naples are the Pontine islands, Ischia and Capri. There's nowhere to anchor on Capri and in the summer the marina fees are extortionate, so we just sailed round it on the way to somewhere cheaper.

On the south side there's a remarkable group of rocks. One of them has a spectacular natural stone arch, that for the local powerboat 'macho men' is the equivalent of the Dunlop bridge at Le Mans.

In the 'Italian Waters Pilot', that essential guide to cruising around Italy and Sardinia, there's a section in the Introduction devoted to Macho Man, to whom Rod Heikell delivers a literary cuff round the ear.

Italian (indeed Mediterranean) macho men can be seen, heard and felt thrashing their power boats around otherwise peaceful spots just about everywhere around the Med, leaving us poor sailing yachties wallowing around in their wake and spilling our tea.

We're not jealous… honest.

UFOs spotted in Salerno harbour

The great thing about Italian ports is that by law they must have a 'transito' quay, *free* for visitors for one or two nights. In Salerno we pushed our luck and stayed for a week, going off to see Naples by train each day.

Like every town quay, Salerno harbour comes complete with the ubiquitous Fishing Family. They sit quietly all day as Papa, his expression impassive and unchanging, drops his hook between cans, bottles, dead fish, lumps of polystyrene foam, and other UFOs.*

*Unidentifiable Floating Objects.

Who needs a big yacht to enjoy a bit of a day sail?

In August, the coast around Salerno is prone to thunderstorms and sudden short vicious squalls which come out of the blue (well, the dark purply gray) and smack you between the eyes.

We were hit by a particularly vicious one, and while we were frantically scrabbling the sails down and heading for the nearest bit of shelter, we spotted this local family, probably taking a break from fishing for UFOs in the harbour, nipping out in the pedalo for a bit of nautical fun.

Every week on the Navtex, on which we receive weather, safety and emergency messages, we read about inflatables blown out to sea, drifting dinghies with no occupants, and missing migrants from North Africa. When you get a bit blasé and start to think of the Med as a big lake, it sort of pulls you up short and you think a bit more carefully about things. But at least this lot had pedal power...

The Scary Footballer of Scario

We were in Scario, a pleasant little town with a tiny harbour and a mountain backdrop, situated just about where Italy's ankle starts to curve forward into the top of the foot.

Scario's only internet café consisted of an elderly laptop, even older than the one on Yanina, perched on a rickety wooden table at the back of the local newsagent's shop. We were trying to get all our emailing and weather-checking done in the hour allotted, when the light went dim. It was something big, very very big, blocking the open doorway. It moved into the shop, and there was the biggest, hairiest Italian I've ever seen, wearing only a pair of flip flops and swimming trunks three sizes too small for him.

Hearing English voices, he moved up to us and asked the usual question:

'Eenglish! Where-a you from?' We live out in the sticks so it's always difficult to pin-point where our house is.

'Er… near Manchester.' This provoked the usual response, but with much more gusto.

'Aaaaaaaaaaaaaaahh! Manchester United!'

I've not followed football since the F.A. Cup Final in 1959, when my home team, Nottingham Forest, won with only ten men in the second half. After that anything would be an anticlimax.

So we prepared to offer our usual bland non-football-fan smiles, but clearly this was going to be a different kind of encounter. His eyes widened, eyebrows raised, mouth formed a perfect 'O', from which a kind of stream-of-consciousness flurry of words emerged.

'SirAlexaFerguson! IyamfootballerIyavaplayforRealMadridIyava-dacupIshakeadahandofaKingofSpainIwritetoSirAlexahenoreplyyou-wannaseedacupIgetafromaKingofSpain?'

'Er…we're a bit busy but…er..'

'Younowannaseedacup?' he said in an incredulous tone, eyebrows raised to new heights.

'Well…if you've got it with you…'

He held a hand up. 'Due minuti.' He dashed outside, kicked his Vespa into life and buzzed off. I looked at the newsagent, who shrugged.

'He crazy crazy man, you justa say yes he no problem.'

We turned back to our emails, hoping for a quick getaway. The doorway

darkened for a second time. We were trapped. From a sports bag our footballer pulled a huge silver cup, a proper football special with two big handles, albeit a bit tarnished and dented.

With a flash of teeth and a flourish he raised it aloft.

'Give-a to me by da King of Spain look-a see my name.'

We talked for a while, admired his cup, and edged toward the door.
He thrust a piece of paper into my hand.

'You get back to Manchester you give-a my number to Sir Alex.'
He followed us out of the shop. 'Look I show you.'

He pulled a tennis ball out of his bag, threw it up in the air, and
kept it there, bouncing it off his forehead, his foot, his knee, back to his
head. He kept it up along the road, the harbour quay, and all the way to the
boat, and it was only by trying to talk at the same time that he finally let
the ball drop into the sea. It was a dazzling display. We said our goodbyes
and climbed aboard, promising faithfully that without fail, the next time
we saw Sir Alex Ferguson, we would *definitely* pass on his phone number… which we still plan to do.

Stromboli and the Aeolians

After Scario, you're really down on the upper slope of Italy's foot, and if you don't stop coast-hopping soon, you'll get to Sicily and you'll have missed Stromboli and the Aeolians. Sounds like an Italian neo-punk band, but in fact it's a group of volcanic islands, and Stromboli is definitely their star performer, producing a small eruption every 20 minutes without fail (you're probably thinking you know several people like that).

In the 'Italian Waters Pilot' this whole area is called the Aeolian Triangle because of the freaky weather conditions that can blow up without warning. Having been scared in Scario, we were more scared now. But as they say, the only thing you have to fear is fear itself. That and an erupting volcano.

We decided to sail overnight past Stromboli and reach the other islands at daybreak. There was no moon, so the only light was starlight, plus the odd cruise ship on the horizon. We knew that we were close and we strained our eyes trying to see a black lump of rock set against a black sky.

Then Stromboli obliged and spat out a sizeable shower of flaming lava. The effect, as an American yachtie friend would say, was 'awesome' and yes, regular, three times an hour. As we passed, a shower of shooting stars scratched their way down the diamond black sky.

'Awesome' sort of covers it, I think.

Photographing Stromboli

Using an early digital camera slower than a box Brownie to photograph Stromboli at night proved to be harder than we thought. Every shot was just three or four red blobs in a totally black background. Couldn't see Stromboli. Meant nothing. So here's the best way...

The Bastardi of the Strait of Messina

The Med is pretty much non-tidal, we all know that. But there are places where the current changes direction enough times a day to be called a tide. The Strait of Messina, which separates Sicily from the mainland, is one, and you have to use the Tide Tables for Gibraltar to get through it.

Odysseus (OK, that's the only time I'll mention him) had a jolly time here. On one side of the Strait was Scylla, a frightful old hag (no, no, not Cilla), who used to pull passing sailors. Off their ships that is. She had six pairs of legs and six horrible heads (more like the Nolans maybe). On the other side was Charybdis, a huge swirling whirlpool which sucked ships down into the dismal deep. All legend of course.

But the 'Italian Waters Pilot' does warn of the 'tagli', tidal bores occurring just after the tide turns, accompanied by high breaking seas and 'bastardi', whirling eddies that can 'bother' a yacht. Throw in a few violent squalls, two or three cargo ships breathing down your neck, high speed ferries crossing your path, and …

'Look,' said Liz, 'don't be so melodramatic. It's only the Raz de Seine with pasta. Just get on with it. I promise the bastardi won't get you.'

The harbour wall, Siracusa, Sicily

Well, the bastardi didn't get us, and neither did Cilla or the Nolan Sisters. But Siracusa's harbour wall did, with a lot of help from us. After the Strait, the harbour wall in Siracusa's Grand Harbour seemed a benevolent sort of place to spend the night. Here we learned a valuable lesson. Read the Pilot, and read it in great detail. Then act on what you just read, in just the way that we didn't. When the wind changed, as we knew it would, we were being blown onto the wall.

'Mediterranean mooring' means that when you want to tie up to a quay, you don't lie alongside it, there's usually no room. Instead you come in at right-angles to the quay. We always come in forwards, halting our progress by flinging out a small anchor, known as a 'kedge', from the back. As we hauled on this to get Yanina away from the wall, we had a long line on the bow that we slowly fed out to stop us from swinging into the boat next door.

Then it all went horribly wrong.

We were making a fine job of ploughing up the sea bed with our kedge anchor, but in that wind Yanina was going nowhere. Error of judgement was then closely followed by total cock-up. Somehow in the next few seconds we got a line round our propeller, stopping the engine, and Yanina crunched her nose against the wall. In my wisdom I had removed the two small nose fenders - wouldn't need them in the anchorage, would we? The wind turned her slowly alongside the wall, and if next door's crew hadn't been ready with some big fat fenders, she would have happily rubbed her topsides up and down the concrete, like a pig scratching its back on a fence.

So what to do next? I suggested finding the nearest café, sitting down for a coffee and working out a decision-making matrix to determine the optimum solution to resolve our problem, but before Liz could offer a reasoned and cogent argument why we should adopt a different strategy, the Coast Guard decided for us, shouting from their motorboat.

'Get on board! Take-a da line!'

We said goodbye to our kedge anchor and chain, and they towed us to the anchorage where we dropped the hook. There they left us, in a rising wind, a line round the prop, and an urgent need for a pair of brown trousers. The next morning in a flat calm, I dived in and freed the prop. We dinghied over to the scene of the crime with a line and one of those small folding grapnel anchors that you buy at boat jumbles and then never use. We used it now.

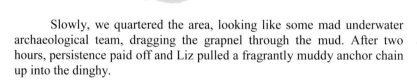

Slowly, we quartered the area, looking like some mad underwater archaeological team, dragging the grapnel through the mud. After two hours, persistence paid off and Liz pulled a fragrantly muddy anchor chain up into the dinghy.

On the end of it was our kedge anchor.

September in Sicily... but where next?

It was late September again and we were looking for a winter berth. We'd been aiming at Tunisia (again) but were told that it was full up, all of it. Malta ('Malta? You must be joking. We're not going there.') was close by. We did a quick, unemotional, rational checklist of plus points for Tunisia and Malta. Result: Malta 7, Tunisia 1.

So Arrivederci Italia (and Corsica, Sardinia, Spain, Portugal and France) and thanks for everything, although not a lot in Sardinia's case. Maybe when you go you'll do better. It's late September and we're off to Malta now. They speak English, they drive on the left, and they've got fish and chips with curry sauce. And when we get fed up with all that, there's Greece and Turkey, and if we're really keen, Syria, Lebanon, Israel, Egypt, Libya, the Red Sea, you don't have to stop. But that's another story.

The route

Not to be used for navigational purposes

Another story
or why you should buy another book just like this one

Yes, it really is another story. 'Right on the nose' is the shocking exposé of our exploration of the Eastern Mediterranean in Yanina, from Malta to Turkey and back. Its winds (yes, just the three), its waters (just as lumpy), and its people (not quite so lumpy). We met mainly Greeks and Turks, who have rubbed shoulders and mingled in these parts for centuries, divided only by the call of the muezzin and their response to a pork souvlaki.

Cruising in Yanina, we gave the Adriatic a miss, because we'd already been there crewing on a delivery trip during the Kosovo crisis. Three days motoring into headwinds, up to 7 metre waves and surrounded by NATO warships, helicopters and submarines. Mmmm.

The Maltese are a happy mixture. They started off, three or four thousand years ago, as expatriate Sicilians, but now they are a blend of nationalities, including those of probably all the seamen who ever stopped in Grand Harbour for more than a day. Apart from the Turks. They haven't been back since 1565 when Grand Master de Vallette saw them off. You see, you get a history lesson too.

And then Tunisia. We finally got there. Not strictly in the Eastern Med, but it looks to the East, its religion is Islam, and it comes over as a bit of a North African Turkey with camels. The people are just as generous and just as much fun.

And what else? Fun with holding tanks, Mediterranean wildlife, a fractured collarbone, pets on board, laundry tips, cruising characters, another marina band, the mirth and excitement just goes on and on...

So when 'Right on the nose' comes out, buy it. There's no more Harry Potter so you may as well. And we've got to get to the Caribbean sooner or later so I'll still need the money.

Saltyspeak a glossary for dirt dwellers

Bavaria	Modern mass-produced yacht
Bilge	The space under the floor that fills with water, dead rats, hair, crumbs and navel fluff
Boom	Holds your sail out, like an upside down curtain rail
Cala	Small Spanish bay
Concrete boat	It really is what it says. Posher term is ferro-cement
Coptic Storm Calendar	Ancient Greek and Turkish weather forecasting system
Dirt dwellers	Landlubbers
Fenders	Inflatable sausage-shaped bumpers
Forts raffalés	Strong gusts of French wind, usually a bit garlicky
Galley	Kitchen in a boat
Grapnel	Small folding anchor with four hooks
GRIB files	Computer data for weather forecasting
Heads	Toilet in a boat
Helm	Where you steer the boat
Inmarsat	Satellite communication for big boats
Junk-rig	A boat with sails like Roman blinds, as used on Chinese junks
Keel	The heavy stabilising blade under the boat
Ketch	Yacht with two masts
Luffing	Steering up into the wind while sailing
Meltemi	Strong Greek summer wind, blows for days
Mistral	Strong French summer wind, blows for days
Nav	Working out your route for tomorrow
Pillars of Hercules	Ancient name for Gibraltar and Ceuta
Pulpit	Stops you falling off the bow
Rias	Beautiful rivers in Northwest Spain
RIB	Hard-bottomed dinghy with inflatable sides
Rigging	Everything that holds up the mast and boom
Shore power	When you plug into electricity in a marina
Spring off a berth	Cunning way of catapulting your boat off the dock when the wind's blowing you on
Springs	The time of the month when the tide rises to its highest, and drops to its lowest
SSB	Short wave radio as used by radio hams
Stanchion	Pole to keep guard rail up. Sort of a hi-tech fencepost
Stateroom	Posh name for a cabin (bedroom) on a big boat
Stern gland	Lets your prop shaft turn but keeps the sea out
Tide Tables	Tell you when the tide's in or out
Topsides	Sides of the boat outside the guard rail
Triremes	Ancient Roman yachts
Windlass	Helps you pull the anchor up while doing your back in

112

References

Cunliffe, Tom, Yachtmaster, author of many books and articles on all aspects of sailing, including anchoring

Garvey, Geoff & Ellingham, Mark, *The Rough Guide to Andalucia*, published by Penguin, 2006

Heikell, Rod, *Italian Waters Pilot*, published by Imray Laurie Norie & Wilson Ltd, 2006

Heikell, Rod, *Mediterranean Cruising Handbook*, published by Imray Laurie Norie & Wilson Ltd, 2004

Lawrence, D. H., *Sea and Sardinia*, Penguin Classic, 1999

McGoohan, Patrick, starred in *The Prisoner*, ITV television series, 1967-8

Milligan, Spike, *I must go down to the sea again, the lonely sea and sky. I left my shoes and socks there, I wonder if they're dry?* I can't confirm this, but I think it came from one of Spike's 'Q' series TV programmes. It is of course based on John Masefield's poem *Sea Fever* of 1878.

Newby, Eric, *On the Shores of the Mediterranean*, published by Picador (Pan Books Ltd), 1984

Acknowledgements

Thanks for inspiration, hard work, help, observations and advice go to the following people:

Liz Cooper, Eric and Dorothy Buxton, Spike Milligan, Patricia Eve, Rod and Lu Heikell, Andrew Morley, Nicky Clarke, Michael Shaw, Kay and Pete, Jim and Katie, Rick and Bonnie, Martha, Alan and Doreen, and everyone who bought our Christmas cards or who commissioned a cartoon.

Thank you for your support.

I shall always wear it.